Australian Outback Food Chains

Bobbie Kalman & Hadley Dyer

🍄 Crabtree Publishing Company

www.crabtreebooks.com

Australian Outback Food Chains

Created by Bobbie Kalman

Dedicated by Bonna Rouse
To my sister Gail, my tower of strength.

Editor-in-Chief
Bobbie Kalman

Writing team
Bobbie Kalman
Hadley Dyer

Substantive editor
Kathryn Smithyman

Project editor
Michael Hodge

Editors
Molly Aloian
Robin Johnson
Kelley MacAulay

Design
Katherine Kantor
Margaret Amy Salter (cover)

Production coordinator
Heather Fitzpatrick

Photo research
Crystal Foxton

Consultant
Patricia Loesche, Ph.D., Animal Behavior Program, Department of Psychology, University of Washington

Illustrations
Barbara Bedell: pages 3 (wombat, bilby, and kangaroo), 11 (kangaroo and wombat), 13 (roots), 25 (bacteria), 27 (kangaroo, wombat, and bilby), 31
Katherine Kantor: pages 3 (grass), 9 (grass), 11 (tree-right and grass), 25 (detritus and soil background in magnifying glass), 28 (fox)
Bonna Rouse: pages 3 (all except wombat, bilby, grass, and kangaroo), 7, 9 (wallaby and dingo), 10, 11 (all except kangaroo, wombat, grass, and tree on right), 13 (tree), 18, 20, 22, 25 (plant), 27 (eagle, plant, butterfly, and ant)
Margaret Amy Salter: pages 25 (magnifying glass), 28 (rabbits)

Photographs
Animals Animals - Earth Scenes: © Prenzel, Fritz: page 12; © Viola, Franklin: page 17 (bottom)
BigStockPhoto.com: Susan Flashman: title page; Amy Halucha: page 22; Gary Unwin: page 23
Paul Bolger, Alice Springs Town Council: page 14 (bottom)
Bruce Coleman Inc.: Frank Krahmer: page 17 (top)
Marc Crabtree: page 31
© Heike Mirabella/Dreamstime.com: page 5 (top)
iStockphoto.com: pages 4, 6 (top), 14 (top), 19
Minden Pictures: Michael & Patricia Fogden: page 15; Mitsuaki Iwago: pages 28-29
Naturepl.com: © Bartussek/ARCO: page 18; © William Osborn: page 24
A.N.T. Photo Library/NHPA: page 6
© ShutterStock.com/Eric Gevaert: page 8
Dave Watts/Tom Stack & Associates: pages 5 (bottom), 7, 21 (top)
Other images by Digital Stock and Digital Vision

Library and Archives Canada Cataloguing in Publication
Kalman, Bobbie, date.
    Australian outback food chains / Bobbie Kalman & Hadley Dyer.

(Food chains)
ISBN-13: 978-0-7787-1950-2 (bound)
ISBN-13: 978-0-7787-1996-0 (pbk.)
ISBN-10: 0-7787-1950-2 (bound)
ISBN-10: 0-7787-1996-0 (pbk.)

    1. Desert ecology--Juvenile literature. 2. Food chains (Ecology)--Australia--Juvenile literature. I. Dyer, Hadley II. Title. III. Series: Food chains

QH197.K34 2006   j577.54'160994   C2006-904125-3

Library of Congress Cataloging-in-Publication Data
Kalman, Bobbie.
    Australian outback food chains / Bobbie Kalman & Hadley Dyer.
        p. cm. -- (Food chains)
    Includes index.
    ISBN-13: 978-0-7787-1950-2 (rlb)
    ISBN-10: 0-7787-1950-2 (rlb)
    ISBN-13: 978-0-7787-1996-0 (pb)
    ISBN-10: 0-7787-1996-0 (pb)
    1. Food chains (Ecology)--Australia--Juvenile literature.
I. Dyer, Hadley. II. Title. III. Series.
    QH197.K334 2007
    577.54'160994--dc22
                                    2006023329

Crabtree Publishing Company

www.crabtreebooks.com   1-800-387-7650

Published in Canada
Crabtree Publishing
616 Welland Ave.
St. Catharines, ON
L2M 5V6

Published in the United States
Crabtree Publishing
PMB16A
350 Fifth Ave., Suite 3308
New York, NY 10118

Published in the United Kingdom
Crabtree Publishing
White Cross Mills
High Town, Lancaster
LA1 4XS

Published in Australia
Crabtree Publishing
386 Mt. Alexander Rd.
Ascot Vale (Melbourne)
VIC 3032

Contents

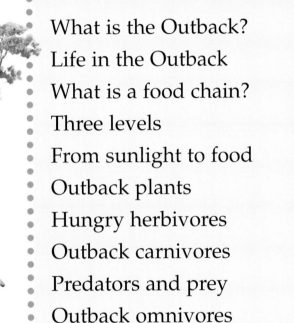

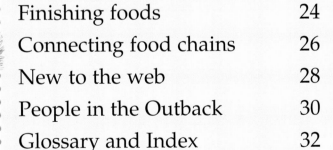

What is the Outback?

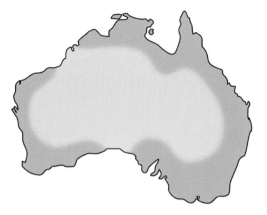

The brown area on this map shows about where the Outback is located within Australia.

The **Outback** is a large area of land in the middle of Australia. It covers about two-thirds of Australia. The Outback has no borders, so people do not agree on exactly where it begins and where it ends.

Hot and dry

The weather in Australia is hot and dry because Australia receives very little rain. It rains less in the Outback than it does in other parts of Australia. When it does rain in the Outback, the rains are very heavy. It does not rain for very long, however. In some parts of the Outback, it may not rain for years! Long periods of time without rain are called **droughts**. During droughts, the soil turns to dust. As a result, **dust storms**, such as the one shown right, sometimes occur in the Outback. Dust storms are strong winds that blow dust around.

Outback deserts

The Outback receives very little rain, so it is made up mainly of **deserts**. Deserts are dry places where few plants grow. Some outback deserts are too dry for any plants to grow. Others have some plants. Most outback desert plants are grasses. **Shrublands** and **woodlands** surround outback deserts. Shrublands are places where grasses, flowering plants, **shrubs**, and a few trees grow. Woodlands are places where many trees grow.

There are not many trees or shrubs growing in the Outback.

Some plants are able to grow in the red sand of the Simpson Desert.

Outback deserts

Three of the largest deserts in the Outback are the Sturt Stony Desert, the Simpson Desert, and the Great Victoria Desert. The ground in the Sturt Stony Desert is covered with small round stones called **gibbers**. The ground in the Simpson Desert is covered mainly by red sand. The ground in the Great Victoria desert is grassy in some places and sandy in other places.

Life in the Outback

After it rains, colorful flowers grow on many desert plants. This Sturt's Desert Pea has bright red flowers.

Outback plants and animals are suited to life in hot, dry places. Plants grow quickly after heavy rains. Most outback plants—and some animals—are able to store water. These plants and animals **absorb**, or take in, a lot of water when it rains. They use the water to survive during droughts. Some desert animals never drink water! They get the water they need from the foods they eat.

Holding water

The water-holding frog is an animal that stores water in its body. When it rains, the frog absorbs water through its skin. When the rain stops, the frog digs into sand or soil. It makes a **chamber**, or hollow space, and stays there until the rain returns. The frog can use its stored water to survive for about two years before it needs more water.

Out at night

Outback weather is hotter in the daytime than it is at night. Many outback animals are **nocturnal**. Nocturnal animals rest during the day and look for food at night. Being nocturnal allows animals to avoid the daytime heat.

Cool kangaroos

During the day, red kangaroos, such as the one above, rest in the shade of trees and shrubs to keep cool. They dig shallow holes under the trees and lie in the cool soil. Red kangaroos also lick the fur on their front legs. The moisture helps keep the animals cool.

Down under

Some animals stay under the ground during the day to avoid the heat. Spinifex hopping mice live in **warrens**, or connected tunnels, under the ground. They stay in their warrens during the day and come out at night to eat.

As soon as the sun goes down, a spinifex hopping mouse leaves its warren to look for food.

7

What is a food chain?

Outback plants and animals are living things. To stay alive, living things need sunlight, air, water, and food. Living things also need **energy**, or power. Plants need energy to grow and to make new plants. Animals need energy to grow, to move, to breathe air, and to find food. Plants and animals get energy from food.

Healthy food

Food contains **nutrients**, or natural substances that keep living things healthy. Plants **produce**, or make, food using energy from the sun. Animals cannot produce food. They must eat other living things to get energy and nutrients.

This central bearded dragon is getting energy and nutrients by eating a grasshopper.

Different foods

Different animals eat different foods to get energy and nutrients. Some animals eat plants. Animals that eat plants are called **herbivores**. **Carnivores** are animals that eat other animals. Some animals eat both plants and animals. They are called **omnivores**.

Creating chains

The pattern that is created when animals eat to get energy and nutrients is called a **food chain**. Every plant and animal belongs to at least one food chain.

Moving energy

All food chains begin with energy from the sun. Green plants absorb the sun's energy and turn it into food. They use some of the energy and store the rest.

sun

plant

When a wallaby eats a plant, it gets only some of the energy that was stored in the plant. The wallaby does not get as much of the sun's energy as the plant received.

wallaby

When a dingo eats a wallaby, energy passes to the dingo through the wallaby. The dingo gets less of the sun's energy than the wallaby received.

dingo

Three levels

Every food chain has three levels. The first level is made up of plants. The second level is made up of herbivores. Carnivores make up the third level.

Level one

Plants are **primary producers**. "**Primary**" means first. Plants make up the first level in a food chain because they produce their own food.

Level two

Herbivores make up the second level of a food chain. They eat food instead of producing it. Herbivores are called **primary consumers** because they are the first living things in a food chain that must **consume**, or eat, food.

Level three

Carnivores make up the third level of a food chain. They are called **secondary consumers** because they are the second group of living things in a food chain that must eat to get energy.

The energy pyramid

Energy moves from plants to herbivores and from herbivores to carnivores. The **energy pyramid** above shows how energy moves in a food chain. The pyramid is wide at the bottom and narrow at the top. There are many plants in a food chain, so the first level of the energy pyramid is the widest level. The second level of the pyramid is narrower because there are fewer herbivores than there are plants in a food chain. The top level of the pyramid is the narrowest because there are fewer carnivores than there are other living things in a food chain.

From sunlight to food

Green plants make their own food using air, sunlight, and water. Making food from air, sunlight, and water is called **photosynthesis**. Green plants contain a **pigment**, or color, called **chlorophyll**. Chlorophyll absorbs energy from the sun. It then combines the sun's energy with water and **carbon dioxide** to make food for the plants. Carbon dioxide is a gas found in air and water. The food plants make is a type of sugar called **glucose**.

These red-and-green kangaroo paws are performing photosynthesis to make food.

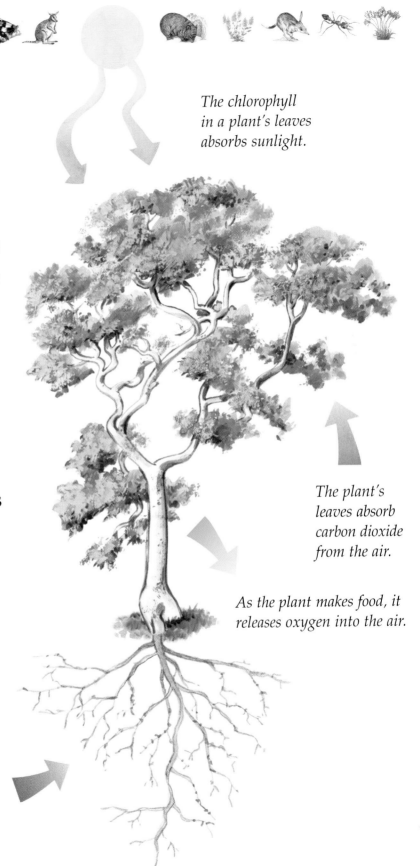

Helpful gases

To survive, plants and animals need to take in different gases from the air. During photosynthesis, plants absorb carbon dioxide from the air. They also release **oxygen** into the air. Animals need to breathe in oxygen to stay alive. Animals breathe out carbon dioxide. Plants provide animals with oxygen, and animals provide plants with carbon dioxide. In this way, plants and animals help each other stay alive.

The chlorophyll in a plant's leaves absorbs sunlight.

The plant's leaves absorb carbon dioxide from the air.

As the plant makes food, it releases oxygen into the air.

The plant's roots absorb water and nutrients from the soil.

Outback plants

Outback plants are suited to hot, dry weather. They have ways of getting the water they need to survive. Most outback grasses are spinifex grasses. Spinifex grasses have hard, narrow, needle-shaped leaves. Their shape allows rain water to run down the leaves and flow directly to the roots in the ground.

*There are dozens of **species**, or types, of spinifex grasses.*

Salty soil

Some outback lakes contain **salt water**. Salt water is water with a lot of salt in it. When a saltwater lake becomes dry, the soil that remains where the lake was is salty. This area of salty soil is called a **clay pan**. Saltbushes are among the few types of plants that can grow in clay pans.

Trees near water

Some outback trees grow near **riverbeds**. Riverbeds are areas where river water flows. When it rains in the Outback, riverbeds fill with water. Some of the river water seeps down into the ground. Water under the ground is called **ground water**. During droughts, the water in riverbeds dries up, but the ground water does not dry up. The trees that grow near riverbeds have long roots that can reach the ground water deep in the soil. Even when there is no water in the riverbed, the trees can get the water they need from the ground water.

When the water in this riverbed dries up, these ghost gum trees can get the water they need from ground water.

Hungry herbivores

Most outback herbivores live in places where plants grow. Certain species of kangaroos, wallabies, and wombats are herbivores that live in the Outback.

Grazing or browsing

Herbivores that eat mainly grasses are known as **grazers**. The southern hairy-nosed wombat is an outback grazer. **Browsers** are herbivores that eat various plant parts, including stems, twigs, buds, leaves, and fruits. Red kangaroos and yellow-footed rock wallabies are browsers.

This baby yellow-footed rock wallaby eats mainly leaves.

Not thirsty

Most outback herbivores drink water from rivers and lakes after it rains. Water is not always available, however. Herbivores can go long periods of time without drinking. Red kangaroos and other herbivores get the water they need from the plants they eat.

Some herbivores eat early in the morning when there is **dew** *on plants. Dew is made up of tiny drops of water. It forms on plants during the night.*

Cool under ground

Southern hairy-nosed wombats are herbivores that live in underground **burrows**. They eat mainly grasses and the roots of shrubs. Wombats store food in their burrows, where the air is **humid**. Humid air contains water. The food the wombats store absorbs some of the water from the humid air. When the wombats eat the stored food, they get the water they need.

Outback carnivores

Many kinds of carnivores live in the Outback. Most outback carnivores are **predators**. Predators are animals that hunt and eat other animals. The animals predators hunt are called **prey**. Most outback predators eat small prey.

Dingoes usually hunt small animals, such as rats and rabbits. This young dingo has caught a lizard.

Secondary and tertiary

When predators hunt and eat herbivores, they are called secondary consumers. A wedge-tailed eagle is a secondary consumer when it eats a herbivore, such as a wallaby. When predators hunt and eat other carnivores, they are called **tertiary consumers**. **"Tertiary"** means "third." Tertiary consumers are the third group of animals in food chains that eat to get energy. The wedge-tailed eagle is a tertiary consumer when it eats another carnivore, such as a bilby.

Healthy populations

Predators are important in food chains because they keep herbivore **populations** healthy. A population is the total number of one species in an area. Predators keep the populations of herbivores healthy and strong by hunting sick, injured, or young animals. These animals are the easiest animals for predators to catch.

Population balance

Predators help keep herbivore populations **balanced**. Having a balanced population means that there is enough food for all the animals to eat. Without predators, herbivore populations would become too large. The herbivores would eventually run out of plants to eat, and they would die. With no herbivores to eat, carnivores would also die.

Short-beaked echidnas are carnivores that eat mainly ants and termites. They stop these insects from eating too many plants.

Predators and prey

Different outback predators have different ways of catching prey. Dingoes usually live alone and hunt small prey. Unlike most outback predators, dingoes sometimes hunt large prey, however. When large prey, such as red kangaroos, are nearby, dingoes form small **packs**, or groups, and work together to hunt the animals.

Finding hidden prey

Perenties, such as the one shown above, eat mice, lizards, insects, and frogs. To find prey, perenties walk with their **snouts** close to the ground. They have parts in their mouths that they use to smell prey hiding under the ground! Perenties use their sharp claws to dig up the prey they have smelled.

Animal defenses

Outback animals have **defenses**, or ways of protecting themselves from predators. Short-beaked echidnas have sharp spines covering most of their bodies. The spines help keep them safe. When a predator bites a prey with spines, it quickly lets go. Being pricked by spines is painful.

Most predators leave echidnas alone!

Run away!

A frilled lizard can scare away predators. The lizard expands the skin around its neck and opens its mouth to make itself look larger. If this surprising action does not scare away the predator, the lizard gets up on its back legs and runs away!

21

Outback omnivores

Many outback animals are omnivores. They eat both plants and animals. Central bearded dragons are omnivores. They eat flowers, fruits, and berries, as well as ants, worms, and snails.

A chance to eat

Most omnivores are **opportunistic feeders**, or animals that will eat any food they can find. Since they eat many kinds of food, outback omnivores have more **opportunities**, or chances, to eat than do carnivores or herbivores.

Central bearded dragons are opportunistic feeders. They have large stomachs, so they eat a lot of food when they find it.

22

Emu menu

Unlike most omnivores, emus are picky eaters. They look for foods that have a lot of nutrients. Emus eat mainly seeds, fruits, flowers, and new leaves. Emus find these foods in the Outback only after a heavy rainfall.

They will not eat dry grass or old leaves, even when these foods are available. Emus follow the rain! When an area begins to dry up, emus move to another place where it has just rained, searching for the plant parts they like to eat.

When no new plants are available, emus may eat insects, lizards, or mice.

Finishing foods

Many outback carnivores are also **scavengers**. Scavengers eat **carrion**, or dead animals. Scavengers are important animals in food chains. By eating dead animals, scavengers help keep their **habitats** clean. Wedge-tailed eagles fly high in the air looking for live animals to eat, such as rabbits, lizards, and birds. These eagles also eat carrion, however. They eat the parts of dead animals that other predators leave behind. The eagle above has found a dead kangaroo to eat.

Leftover energy

After they die, plants and animals **decompose**, or break down. Decomposing plants and animals are called **detritus**. **Bacteria** and some animals eat detritus. Living things that eat detritus are called **decomposers**. Decomposers get energy and nutrients from detritus. They then release some of the nutrients into the soil.

A detritus food chain

This **detritus food chain** shows how energy moves from detritus to plants.

When a plant or animal dies, it becomes detritus in the soil.

Decomposers in the soil, such as these bacteria, eat the detritus. The bodies of decomposers release nutrients from the detritus into the soil.

Note: The arrows point toward the living things that receive nutrients.

The nutrients in the soil help plants grow.

Connecting food chains

There are many food chains in the Outback. A single food chain is made up of plants, a herbivore, and a carnivore. When an animal from one food chain eats a plant or an animal from another food chain, the food chains connect. Two or more connecting food chains form a **food web**. Many outback animals eat different kinds of foods. These animals belong to different food webs.

This dingo belongs to several food chains because it eats many kinds of prey.

An outback food web

This diagram shows a food web in the Outback. The arrows point toward the living things that receive food energy.

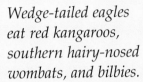

Wedge-tailed eagles eat red kangaroos, southern hairy-nosed wombats, and bilbies.

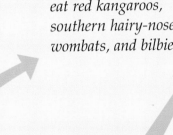

Red kangaroos eat plants.

Southern hairy-nosed wombats eat plants.

Bilbies eat bulldog ants and plants.

Wood white butterflies eat plants.

plants

Bulldog ants eat plants and wood white butterflies.

New to the web

Australia is a **continent**. Many people have moved to Australia from other continents. Some of these people brought animals with them. They brought horses, camels, and water buffalo as work animals. They also brought animals such as cats to keep as pets, as well as foxes and rabbits to hunt for sport. Animals that are brought to a continent from a different continent are called **introduced animals**.

This 1000-mile-long (1,609 km) fence was built in 1907 to keep rabbits out of the western part of Australia.

Growing populations

Introduced animals became parts of outback food chains by eating outback plants and animals. A few outback animals ate the introduced animals, but many did not. With plenty to eat—and few predators—the populations of introduced animals grew quickly.

Nearly wiped out

Introduced animals have caused populations of **wild** Australian animals to decrease. Rabbit populations in the eastern part of Australia increased quickly until there were millions of rabbits there. The rabbits built underground homes in many of the places where bilbies lived, leaving the bilbies with nowhere to live. Cat and fox populations also increased. Cats and foxes both eat bilbies. Together, these animals nearly wiped out the bilby population in the Outback.

People in the Outback

The actions of people threaten outback plants and animals. Some people **clear** large areas of land for **mines** or farms. Clearing land means removing the plants from it. Most farmers raise **livestock**. Livestock crush burrows and other animal homes as they walk over them. They also eat the plants in an area as they walk. As a result, the herbivores in that area have less food. Some of the herbivores die. When there are fewer herbivores, carnivores have less food. As a result, some carnivores, such as dingoes, hunt and eat livestock. Farmers often **poison**, trap, or shoot the carnivores that eat their livestock. Farmers have killed so many dingoes, that these animals are at risk of becoming **endangered**.

Outback tourists

Thousands of **tourists** visit the Outback every year. Large numbers of tourists can be harmful to animals, however. Many animals are killed by the vehicles used by tourists on outback roads. People also **litter**, or leave garbage, in the Outback. Littering is harmful to animals because they can get sick if they eat the garbage.

One of the most popular places in the Outback for tourists to visit is Ayers Rock.

Hope for the Outback!

Some outback animals, such as bilbies, are endangered. People around the world are working to protect bilbies and other outback animals and their habitats. Some people work with the Australian government to pass laws that prevent people from harming outback animals and their habitats. Other people study outback plants and animals to find new ways to help them survive. You can learn more about the Outback and the plants and animals that live there at the library and on the Internet.

Glossary

Note: Boldfaced words that are defined in the text may not appear in the glossary.

bacteria Tiny living things that break down dead plants and animals

burrow A hole that an animal digs as its home

clear To remove plants from a habitat to make it available to people

continent One of the seven large areas of land on Earth (Africa, Antarctica, Asia, Australia, Europe, North America, and South America)

endangered Describing animals that are in danger of dying out

habitat The natural place where a plant or animal lives

livestock Animals that are raised by people for food

mine An underground area where people dig for metals such as gold

oxygen A gas in air and water that animals need to breathe

poison To give a living thing a substance that can cause it to become sick or to die

shrub A woody plant that is smaller than a tree

snout The nose and mouth of an animal

tourist A person who travels to a place for pleasure

wild Describing plants and animals that live in natural habitats

Index

Printed in the U.S.A.